BILLIE EILISH
FOR UKULELE

ISBN 978-1-5400-9204-5

HAL•LEONARD®

Visit Hal Leonard Online at
www.halleonard.com

Contact us:
Hal Leonard
7777 West Bluemound Road
Milwaukee, WI 53213
Email: info@halleonard.com

In Europe, contact:
Hal Leonard Europe Limited
42 Wigmore Street
Marylebone, London, W1U 2RN
Email: info@halleonardeurope.com

In Australia, contact:
Hal Leonard Australia Pty. Ltd.
4 Lentara Court
Cheltenham, Victoria, 3192 Australia
Email: info@halleonard.com.au

Bad Guy

Words and Music by Billie Eilish O'Connell and Finneas O'Connell

Lead vocal written an octave higher than sung.

Interlude

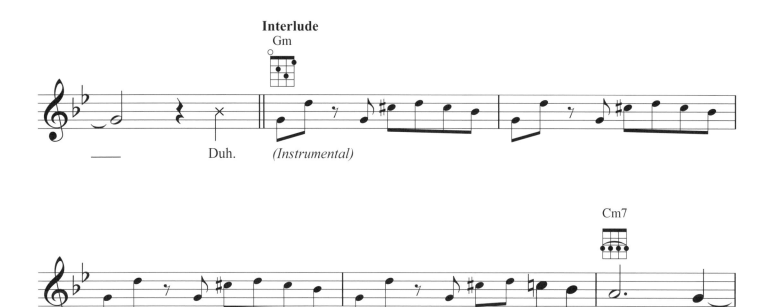

Duh. (Instrumental)

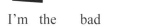 

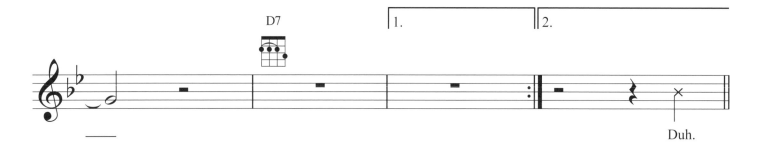

I'm the bad guy. —

— 1.   2.

Duh.

Outro

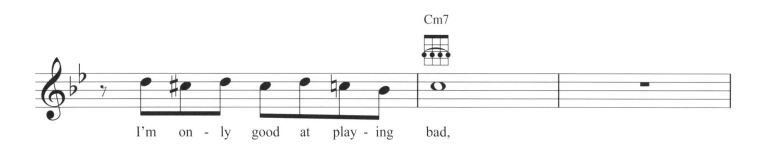

(Instrumental)

I'm on - ly good at play - ing bad,

bad.

4

Hostage

Words and Music by Billie Eilish O'Connell and Finneas O'Connell

I don't _ know what feels true, but this feels right, so stay a
Gold's fake _ and real love hurts, but noth-ing hurts when I'm a -

sec. Yeah, you feel right, so stay a sec.
lone. When you're with me and we're a - lone. And let me

Chorus

crawl _____ in - side your veins. I'll build a

wall, _____ give you a ball and chain. It's not like

me to be so mean, you're all I want - ed. Just let me

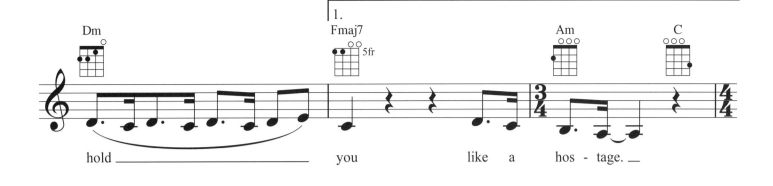

hold _____ you like a hos - tage. __

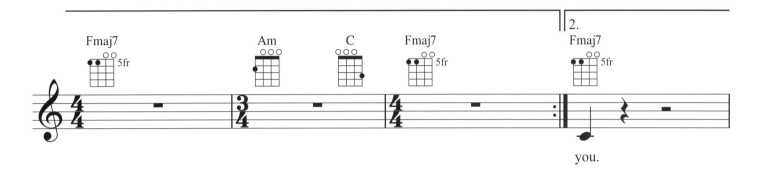

you.

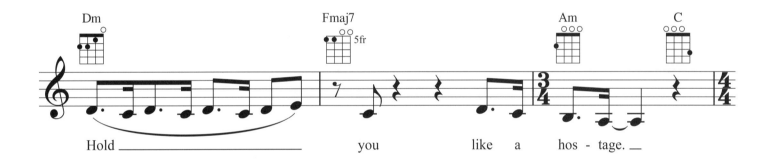

Hold _____ you like a hos - tage. __

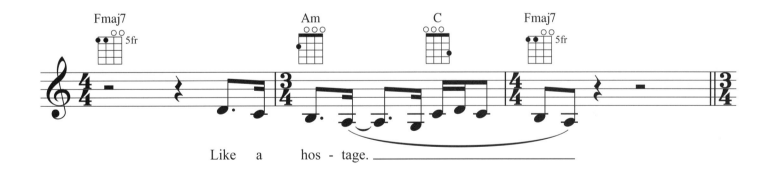

Like a hos - tage. _____

Outro

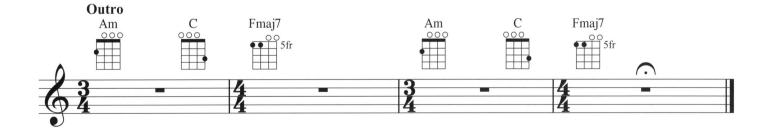

Bellyache

Words and Music by Billie Eilish O'Connell and Finneas O'Connell

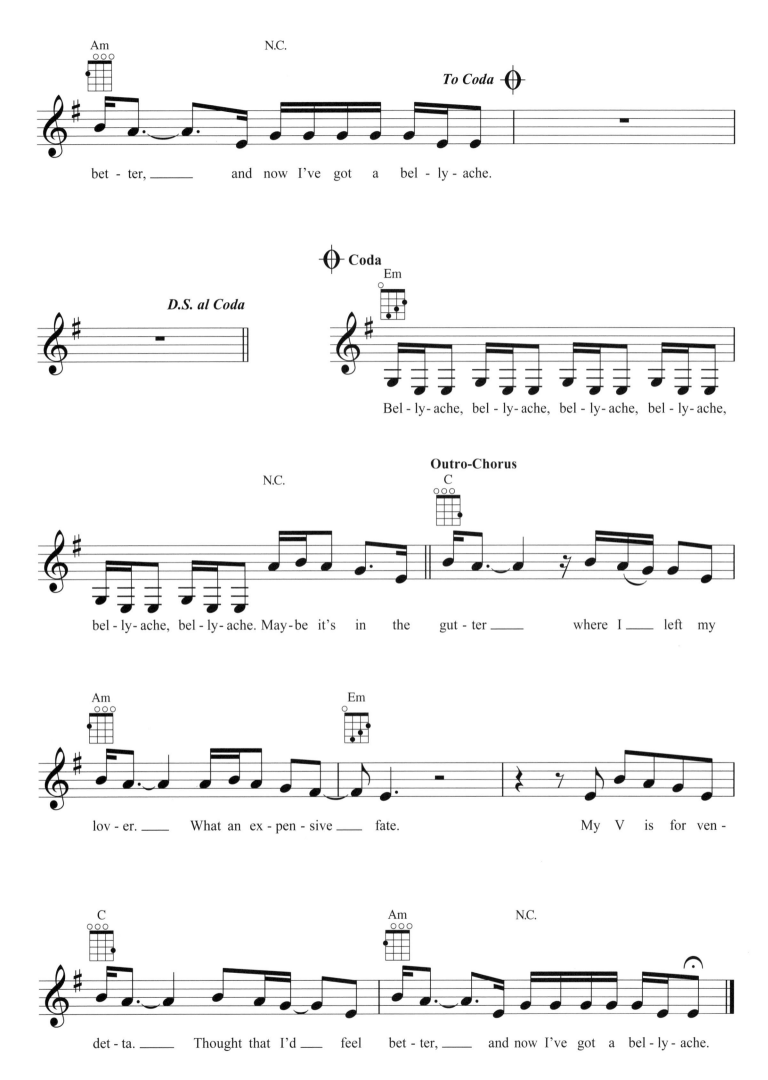

bet - ter, _____ and now I've got a bel - ly - ache.

D.S. al Coda

Coda

Bel - ly-ache, bel - ly-ache, bel - ly-ache, bel - ly-ache,

Outro-Chorus

bel - ly-ache, bel - ly-ache. May-be it's in the gut - ter _____ where I _____ left my

lov - er. _____ What an ex - pen - sive _____ fate. My V is for ven -

det - ta. _____ Thought that I'd _____ feel bet - ter, _____ and now I've got a bel - ly - ache.

Bored

Words and Music by Billie Eilish O'Connell, Finneas O'Connell, Tim Anderson and Aron Forbes

(Bored.)   I'm ___ so bored.

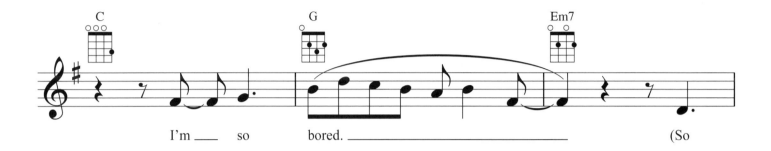

I'm ___ so bored. _____ (So

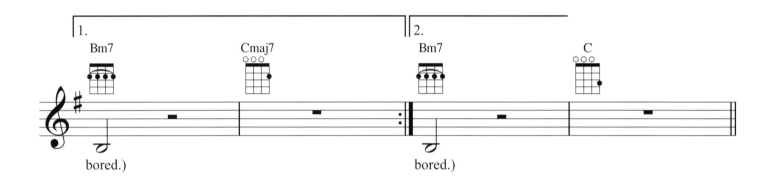

|1.| |2.|

bored.)   bored.)

Pre-Chorus

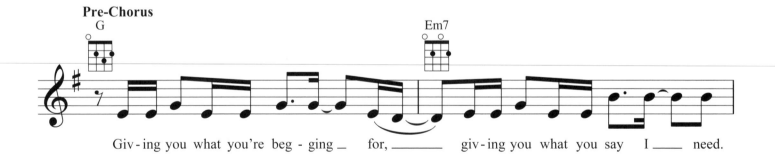

Giv-ing you what you're beg-ging ___ for, _____ giv-ing you what you say I ___ need.

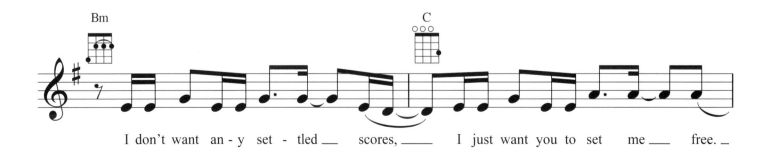

I don't want an-y set-tled ___ scores, ___ I just want you to set me ___ free. _

Giv-ing you what you're beg - ging ___ for, ___ giv-ing you what you say I ___ need,

say I ___ need. ___

Outro-Chorus

I'm not a - fraid an - y - more. ___

What makes ___ you sure ___ you're all I need? ___ For - get a - bout it. ___

And when you walk out the door ___ and leave ___ me torn,

___ you're teach - ing me ___ to live with - out it. ___

Come Out and Play

Words and Music by Billie Eilish O'Connell and Finneas O'Connell

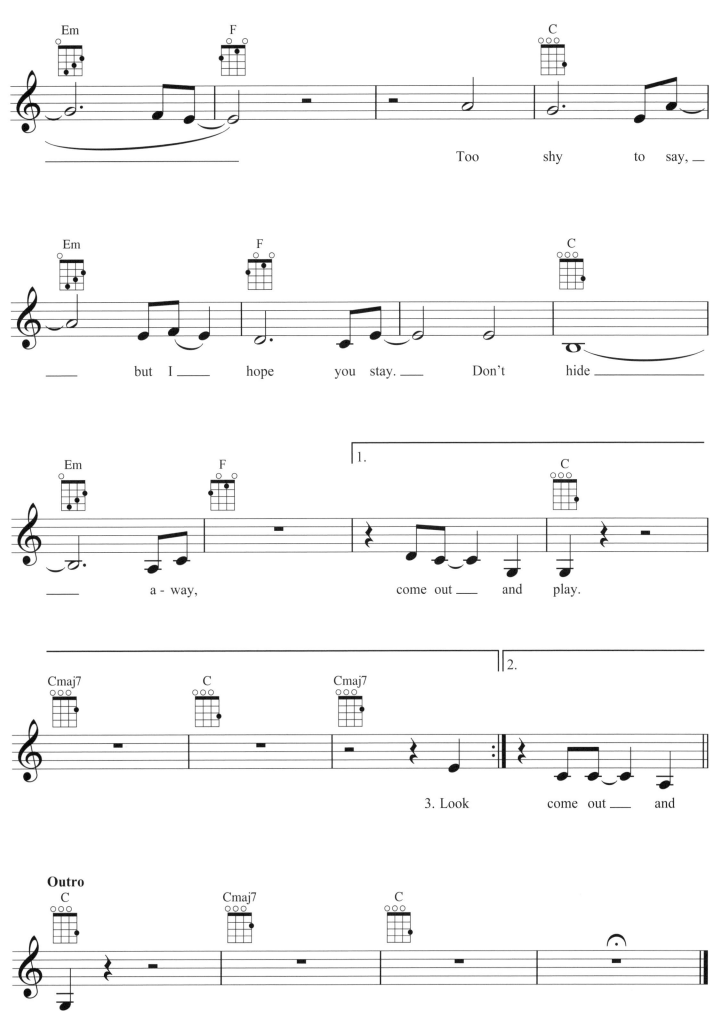

Too shy to say, ___

___ but I ___ hope you stay. ___ Don't hide ___

1.

___ a - way, come out ___ and play.

2.

3. Look come out ___ and

Outro

play.

8

Words and Music by Billie Eilish O'Connell and Finneas O'Connell

To play in original key of E♭ Major, place capo at 3rd fret.

**Vocal written an octave higher than sung.

Interlude

Verse

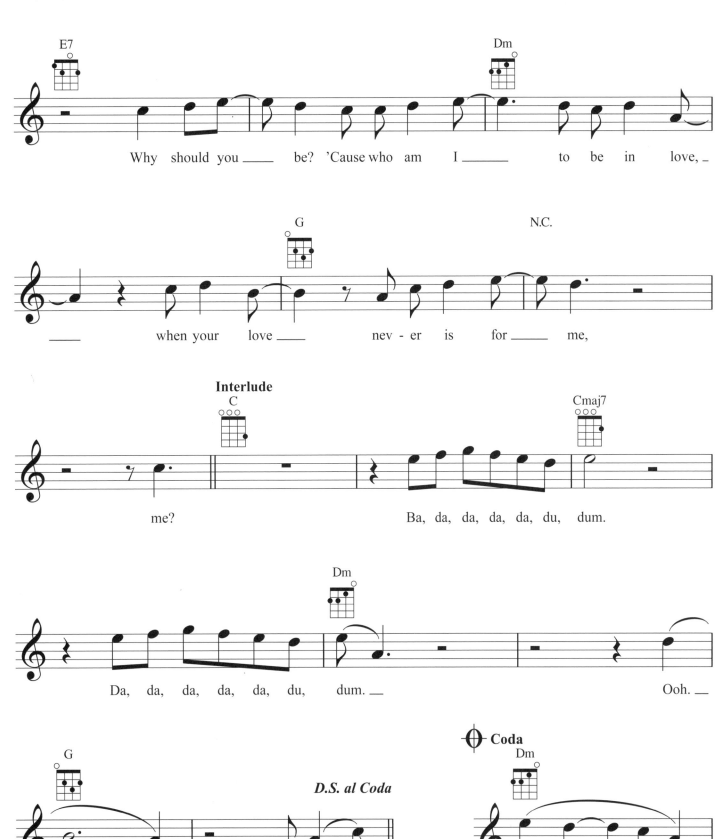

Why should you ___ be? 'Cause who am I ___ to be in love, ___

___ when your love ___ nev-er is for ___ me,

Interlude

me? Ba, da, da, da, da, du, dum.

Da, da, da, da, da, du, dum. ___ Ooh. ___

Coda

D.S. al Coda

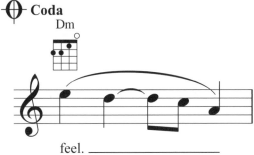

So I ___ feel. ___

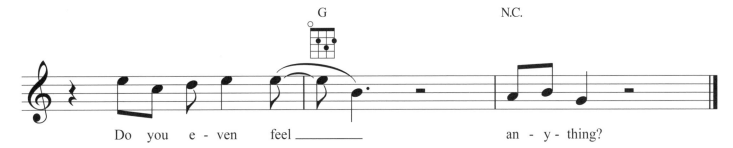

Do you e - ven feel ___ an - y - thing?

23

Everything I Wanted

Words and Music by Billie Eilish O'Connell and Finneas O'Connell

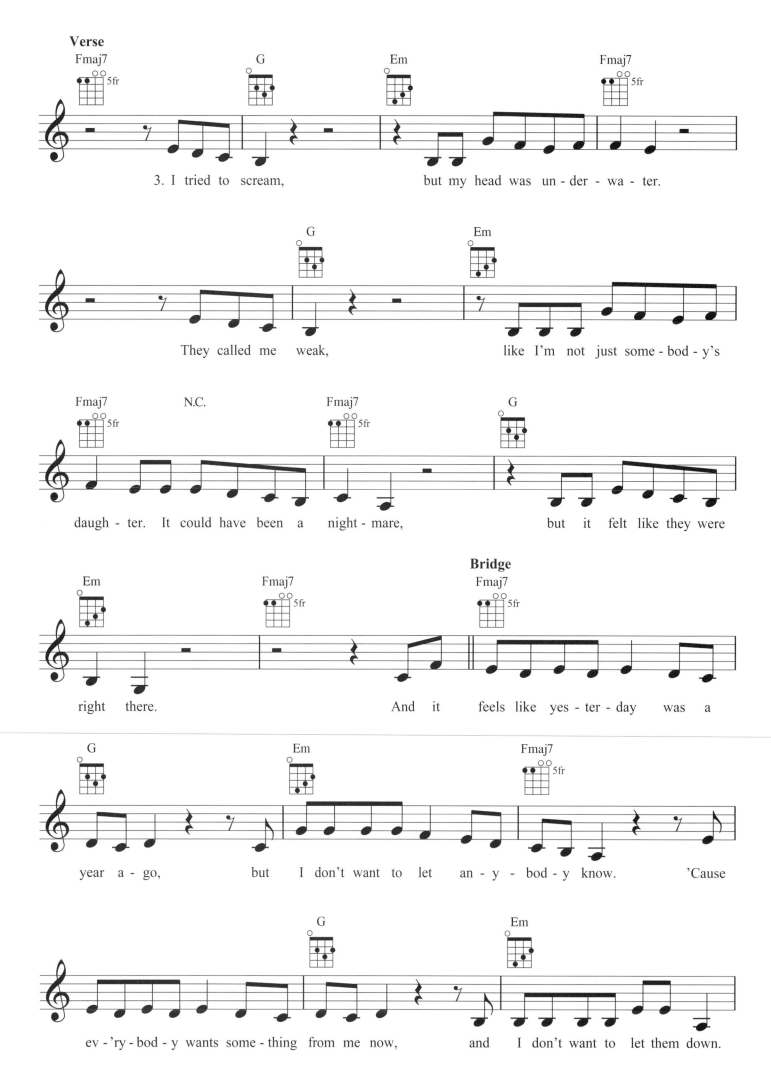

Verse

Fmaj7   G   Em   Fmaj7

3. I tried to scream,   but my head was un - der - wa - ter.

G   Em

They called me weak,   like I'm not just some - bod - y's

Fmaj7   N.C.   Fmaj7   G

daugh - ter. It could have been a night - mare,   but it felt like they were

Bridge

Em   Fmaj7   Fmaj7

right there.   And it feels like yes - ter - day was a

G   Em   Fmaj7

year a - go,   but I don't want to let an - y - bod - y know.   'Cause

G   Em

ev - 'ry - bod - y wants some - thing from me now,   and I don't want to let them down.

idontwannabeyouanymore

Words and Music by Billie Eilish O'Connell and Finneas O'Connell

tight dress __ is what makes you a whore. If "I

love you" was a prom - ise, would you break it ____ if you're hon - est, tell the

mir - ror what you know she's heard be - fore?

To Coda ⊕

I don't wan - na be you ____ an - y -
be you, ____

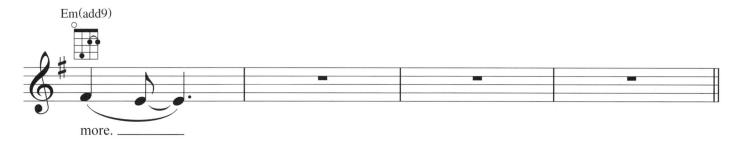

more. _____

Verse

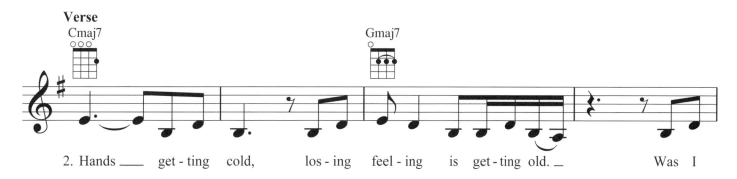

2. Hands __ get - ting cold, los - ing feel - ing is get - ting old. __ Was I

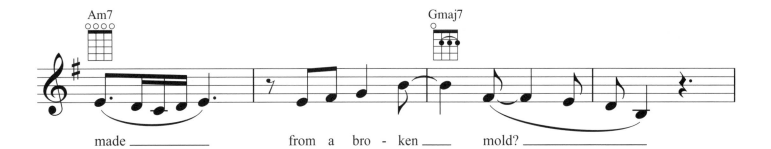

made _____ from a bro - ken ____ mold? _____

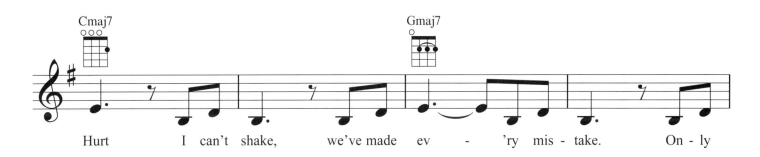

Hurt   I can't shake,   we've made ev - 'ry mis - take.   On - ly

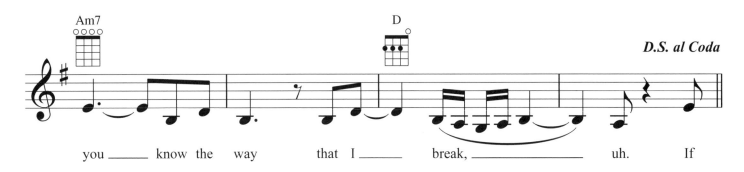

D.S. al Coda

you _____ know the way   that I _____ break, _____ uh.   If

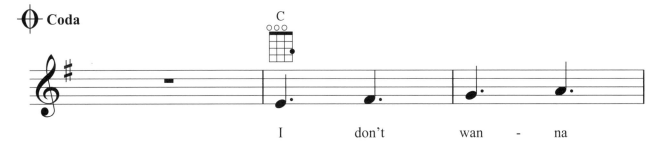

Coda

I   don't   wan - na

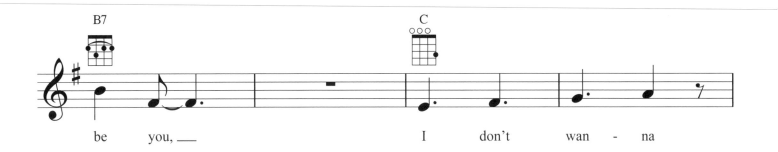

be   you, ___   I   don't   wan - na

be   you ___   an - y - more. ___

Listen Before I Go

Words and Music by Billie Eilish O'Connell and Finneas O'Connell

Verse
Slowly, in 2

1. Take me to the roof - top. I wan - na see the
2. Taste me, the salt - y tears on my cheek. That's

world when I stop breath - ing, turn - ing blue.
what a year - long head - ache does to you.

Tell me love is end - less. Don't be
I'm not o - kay, feel so scat - tered. Don't say I'm

so pre - ten - tious. Leave me like you do.
all that mat - ters. Leave me. Dé - jà vu.

Vocals written an octave higher than sung.

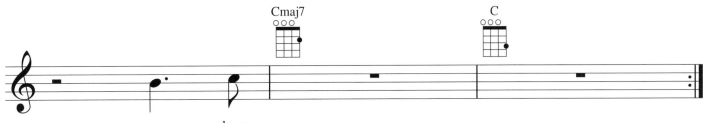

mm,   down.

Outro

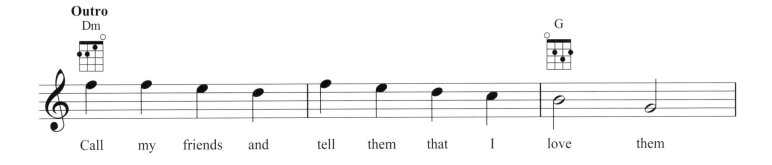

Call   my   friends   and   tell   them   that   I   love   them

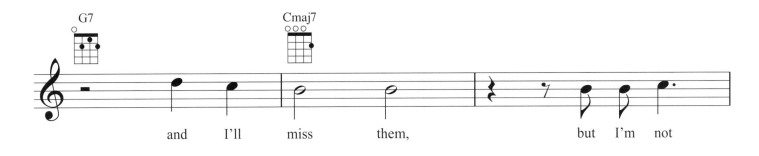

and   I'll   miss   them,   but   I'm   not

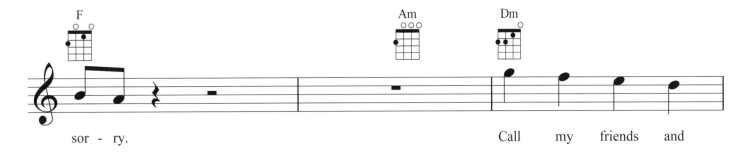

sor - ry.   Call   my   friends   and

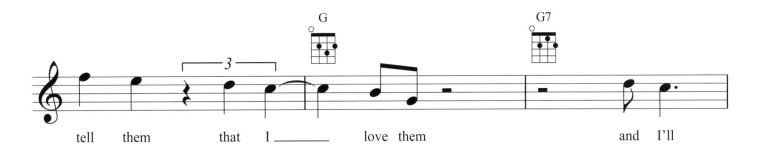

tell   them   that   I _____ love   them   and   I'll

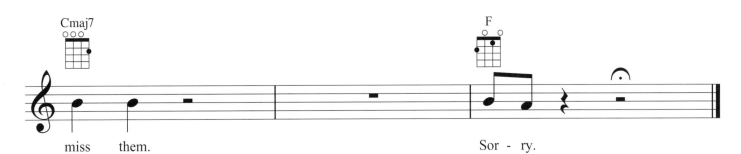

miss   them.   Sor - ry.

I Love You

Words and Music by Billie Eilish O'Connell and Finneas O'Connell

First note

Verse
Moderately

1. It's not true. Tell me I've ___ been lied to.
(2.) all night on an-oth - er red - eye.

Cry - ing is - n't like you. Ooh. _____
I wish we'd nev - er learned to fly, I. _____

What the hell ___ did I _____ do?
May - be we ___ should just ___ try

Nev - er been ___ the type ___ to let some-one ___ see
to tell our - selves ___ a good ___ lie. Did - n't mean ___ to

right through. Ooh. _____
make you cry, I. _____

* Let chord ring.

Ocean Eyes

Words and Music by Finneas O'Connell

First note

Intro
Moderately

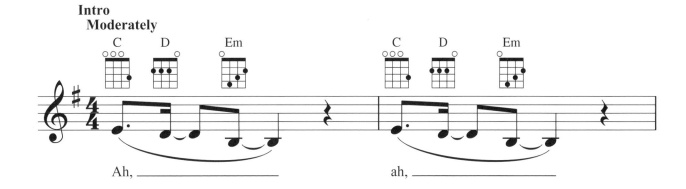

Ah, _____ ah, _____

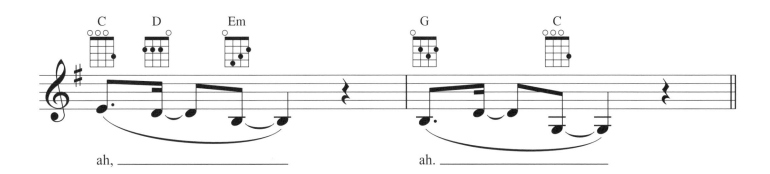

ah, _____ ah. _____

Verse

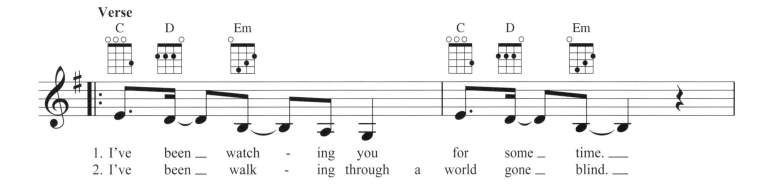

1. I've been _ watch - ing you   for some _ time. _
2. I've been _ walk - ing through a world gone _ blind. _

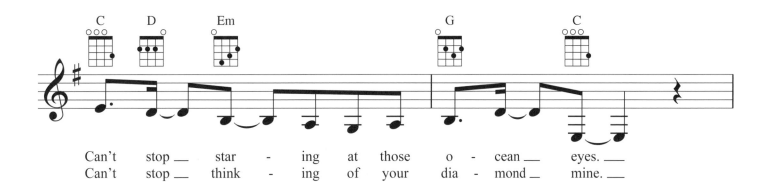

Can't stop _ star - ing at those o - cean _ eyes. _
Can't stop _ think - ing of your dia - mond _ mine. _

Burn - ing ___ cit - ies and na - palm ___ skies. ____
Care - ful ___ crea - ture made friends with ___ time. ____ He

Fif - teen ___ flares ___ in - side those o - cean ___ eyes, ____ your
left her ___ lone - ly with a dia - mond ___ mine ___ and those

𝄋 Chorus

o - cean ___ eyes. ___ }
o - cean ___ eyes. ___ } No fair. _____

_____ You real - ly know how to make ___ me cry ___ when you give me those

o - cean ___ eyes. ___ I'm scared. _____

_____ I've nev-er fall-en from quite __ this high. ___ Fall-ing in-to your

To Coda ⊕

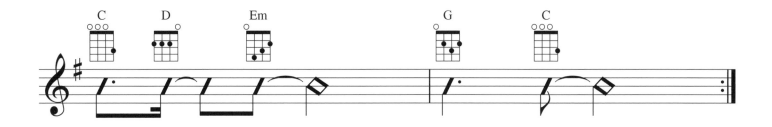

o - cean __ eyes, ___ those o - cean __ eyes. ___

Interlude

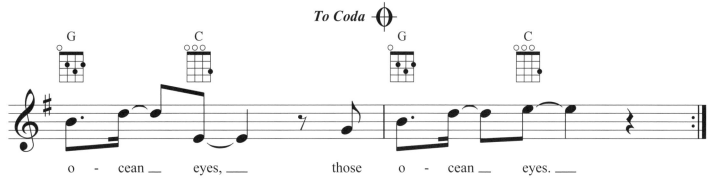

(Vocal ad lib.)

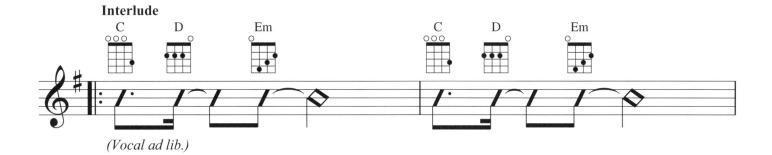

⊕ **Coda**

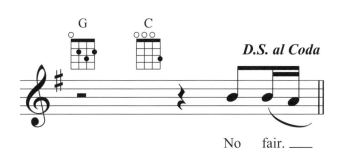

D.S. al Coda

No fair. ___

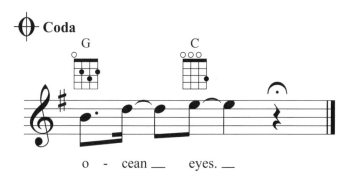

o - cean __ eyes. ___

Lovely

Words and Music by Billie Eilish O'Connell, Finneas O'Connell and Khalid Robinson

hun - dred years. Need a place ___ to hide, but

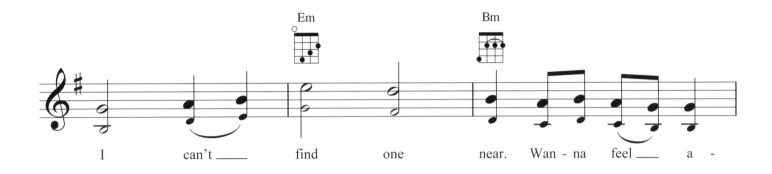

I can't ___ find one near. Wan - na feel ___ a -

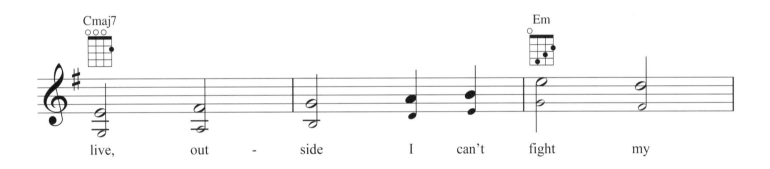

live, out - side I can't fight my

Chorus

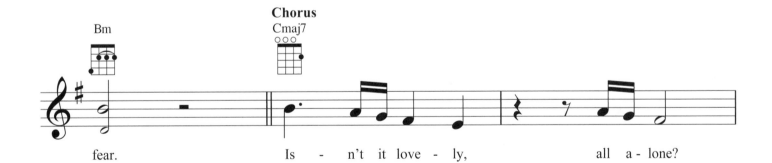

fear. Is - n't it love - ly, all a - lone?

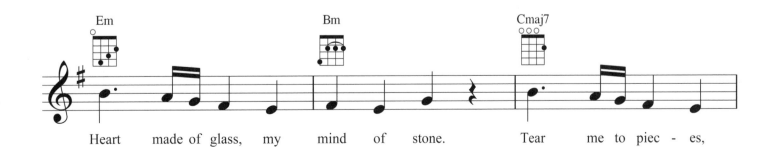

Heart made of glass, my mind of stone. Tear me to piec - es,

skin to bone. Hel - lo, wel - come home.

2. Walk - ing out of time, ____

look - ing for a bet - ter place.

Some - thing's on my mind,

al - ways in my head space. But I know ____ some -

No Time to Die

from NO TIME TO DIE

Words and Music by Billie Eilish O'Connell and Finneas O'Connell

1. I should have known _____ I'd leave a - lone. _

Just goes to show _____ that the blood _

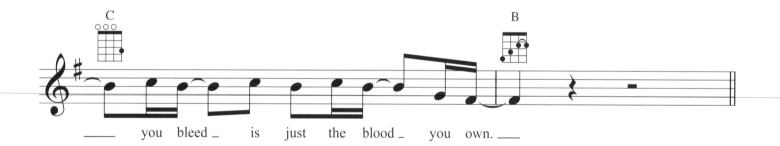

_____ you bleed _ is just the blood _ you own. _

2. We were a pair, _____ but I saw you there, _

* Vocal written one octave higher than sung.

_____ too much to bear. _____ You were _ my life, _

_____ but life ___ is far ___ a - way _ from fair. Was I

Pre-Chorus

stu - pid to love _ you? Was I reck - less to help? _ Was it

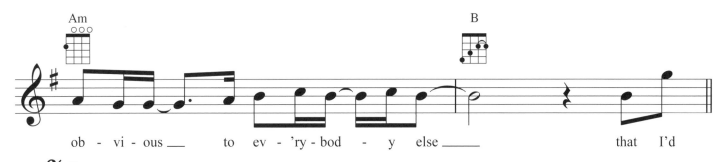

ob - vi - ous ___ to ev - 'ry - bod - y else ____ that I'd

𝄇 Chorus

fall - en for ___ a lie? _____ You were nev - er on ___ my side. _

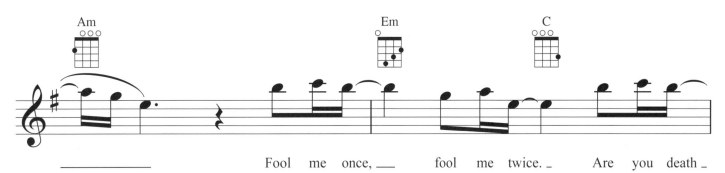

_____ Fool me once, ___ fool me twice. _ Are you death _

Six Feet Under

Words and Music by Finneas O'Connell

First note

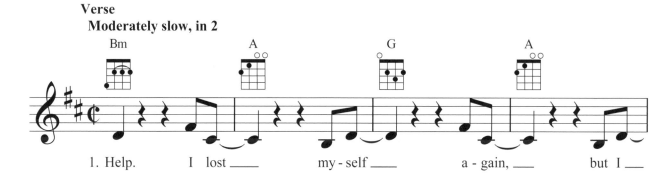

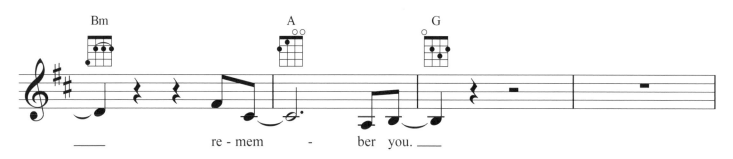

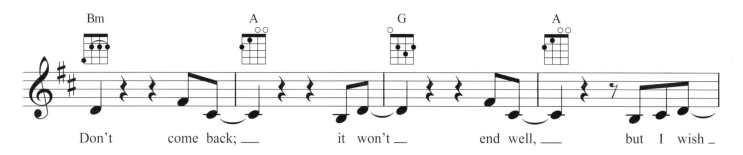

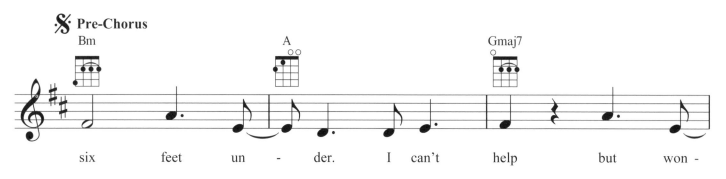

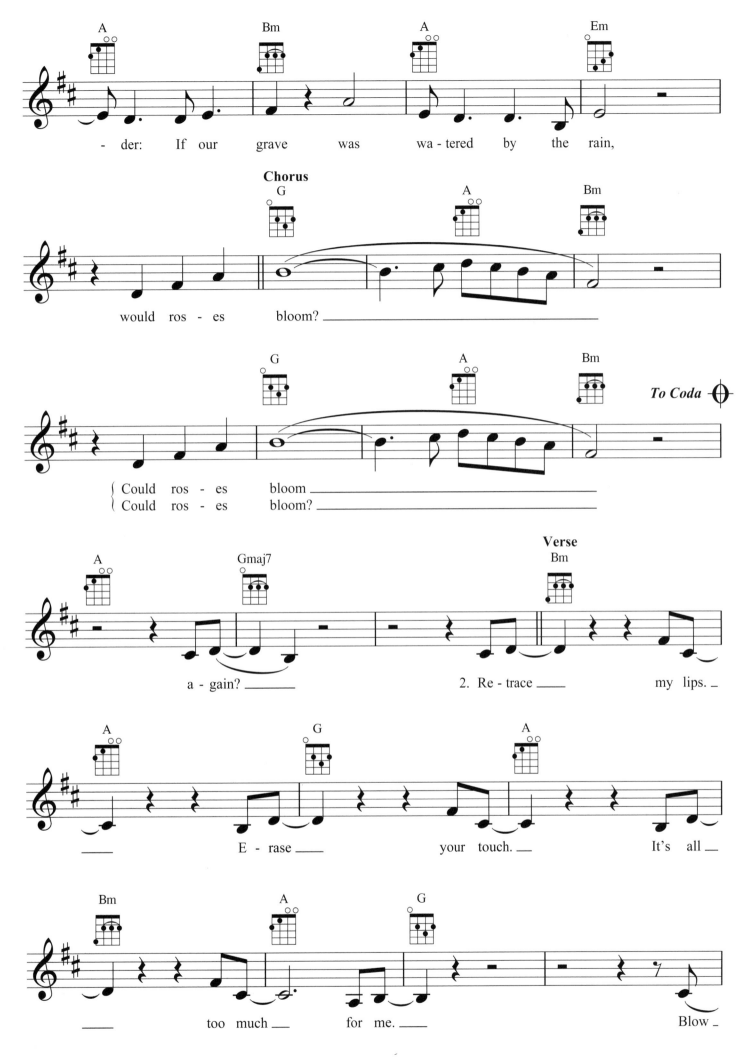

a - way ___ like smoke in air. ___

___ How can you ___ die care - less - ly? ___

Coda

Bridge

N.C.

D.S. al Coda

Our love is

They're play - ing our sound,

lay - ing us down to - night; ___ and

all of these clouds cry - ing us back to life. ___

Pre-Chorus

But you're cold as the ___ night. Six feet un -

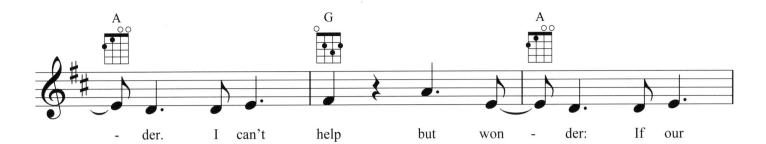

- der. I can't help but won - der: If our

grave was wa - tered by the rain...

Chorus

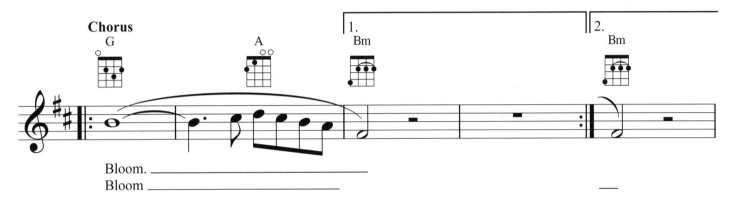

Bloom. _____
Bloom _____ —

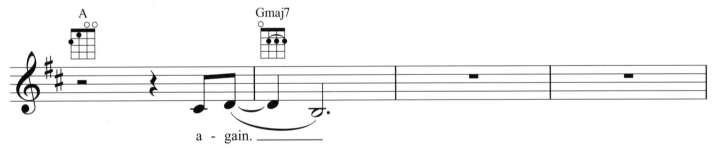

a - gain. _____

Outro-Verse

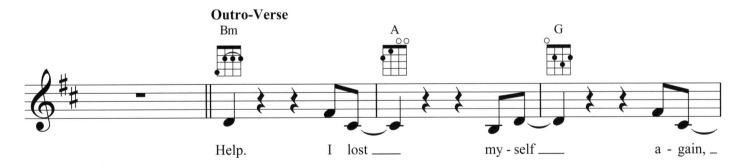

Help. I lost ____ my - self ____ a - gain, _

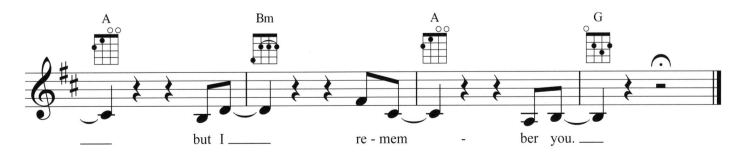

____ but I ____ re - mem - ber you. ____

51

Watch

Words and Music by Finneas O'Connell

with the fi - re that you start - ed in ____ me, but you nev - er came ____

back to ask it out. ____ Go a - head and watch my heart ____ burn _____

with the fi - re that you start - ed in ____ me, but I'll nev - er let you

To Coda ⊕

back to put it out. _____ **Verse** 2. Your love ____ feels so fake ____

_____ and my de - mands ____ aren't ____ high to ____ make. ____ If

I could get to sleep, __ I would have slept by now. Your

lies will nev-er keep, __ I think you need to blow them __ out. __

N.C.

D.S. al Coda

I'll sit and

⊕ Coda

back to put it out. _____

When you call my

Bridge

name, __ do you think I'll come run-ning? You nev-er did the same, __

so good at giv-ing me ___ noth - ing. ___ When you close your eyes, ___

___ do you pic-ture me? ___ When you fan-ta-size, ___ am I your fan-ta-sy? ___ Now you

know, ___ now I'm free. I'll sit and

Chorus

watch your car ___ burn ___ with the fi-re that you start-ed in ___ me,

but you nev-er came ___ back to ask it out. ___

Party Favor

Words and Music by Billie Eilish O'Connell and Finneas O'Connell

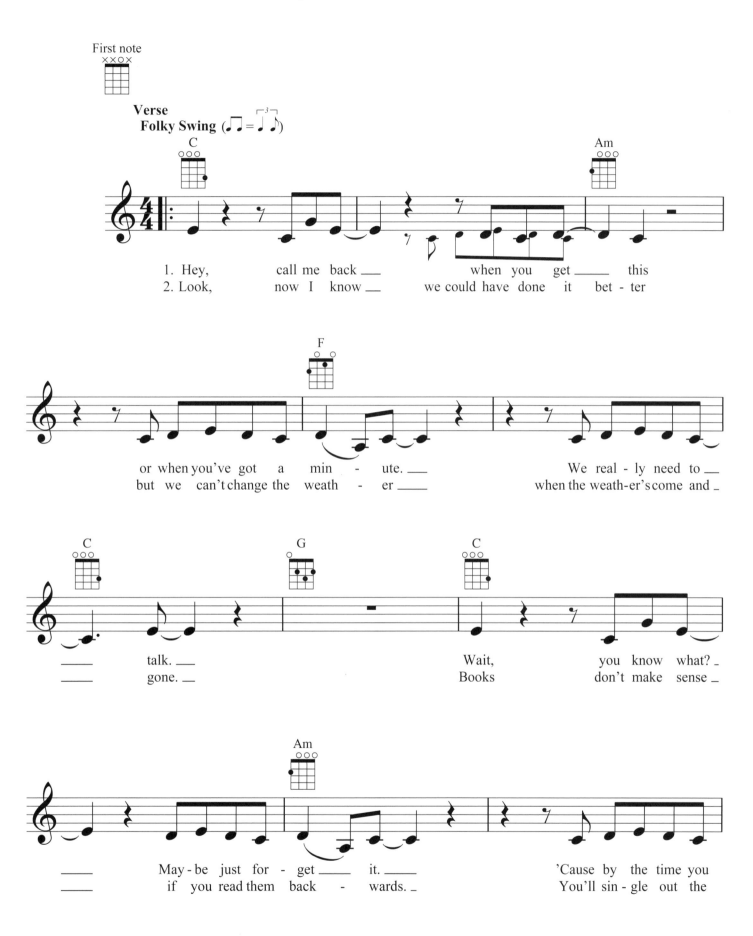

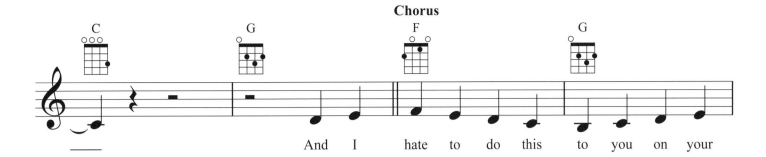

And I hate to do this to you on your

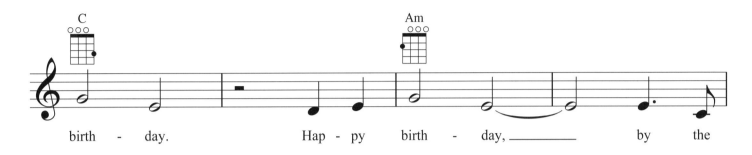

birth - day. Hap - py birth - day, _____ by the

way. "It's not you, it's me" and all that oth - er

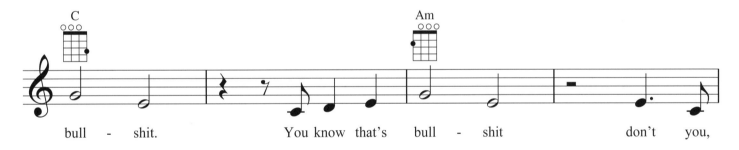

bull - shit. You know that's bull - shit don't you,

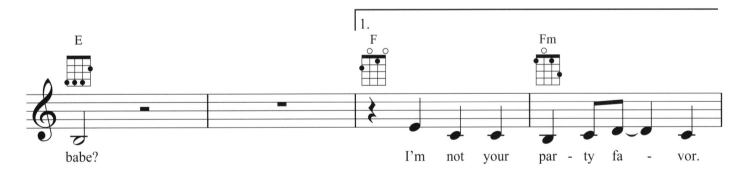

babe? I'm not your par - ty fa - vor.

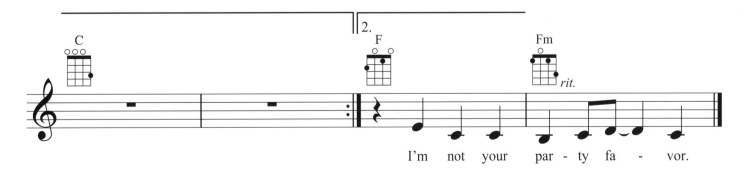

I'm not your par - ty fa - vor.

Wish You Were Gay

Words and Music by Billie Eilish O'Connell and Finneas O'Connell

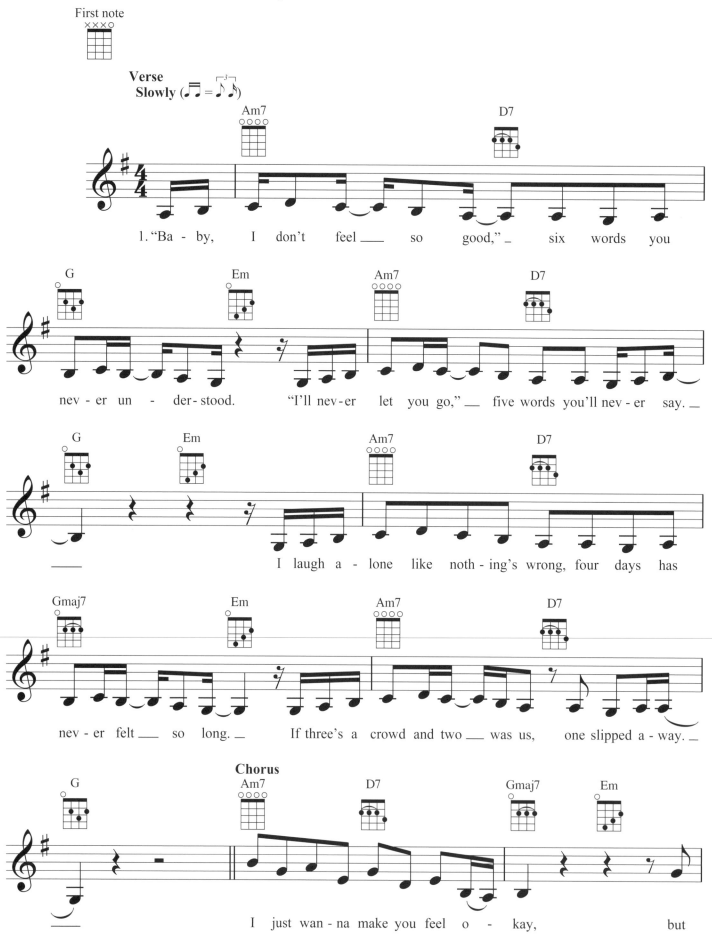

tear - ing out ___ my hair, ___ nine times you nev - er made ___ it there. ___ I ate a -

lone at sev - en, you were six min - utes ___ a - way.

Chorus

N.C.

How'm I s'posed to make you feel o - kay when all you do is walk the oth - er ___

way? Uh. ___ I can't tell you how much I wish I did - n't

wan - na stay, ___ uh. ___ I just kind - a wish you were gay. ___

kay,   but   all   you   do   is   look   the   oth - er   way, __

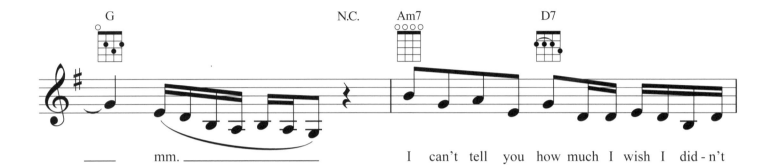

__   mm. _____   I   can't   tell   you   how   much   I   wish   I   did - n't

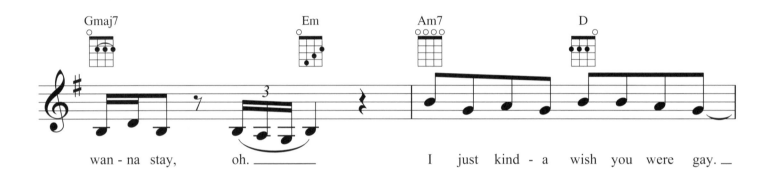

wan - na   stay,   oh. _____   I   just   kind - a   wish   you   were   gay. __

Outro

__   I   just   kind - a   wish   you   were __ gay. __

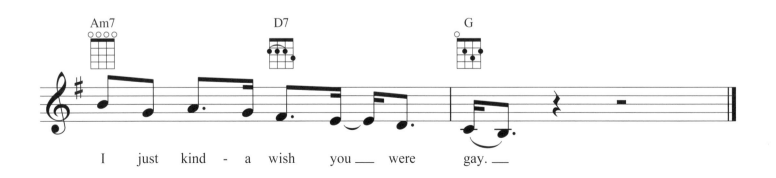

I   just   kind - a   wish   you __ were   gay. __